W9-CAN-886

Profiles of the Presidents

GEORGE W. BUSH

★ ★ ★

Profiles of the Presidents

GEORGE W. BUSH

by Michael Burgan

Content Adviser: Rich McElroy, Historian, McKinley Museum and National Memorial, Grand Rapids, Michigan

Reading Adviser: Dr. Linda D. Labbo, Department of Reading Education, College of Education, The University of Georgia

COMPASS POINT BOOKS ✦ MINNEAPOLIS, MINNESOTA

Compass Point Books
3109 West 50th Street, #115
Minneapolis, MN 55410

Visit Compass Point Books on the Internet at *www.compasspointbooks.com*
or e-mail your request to *custserv@compasspointbooks.com*

Photographs ©: Courtesy of the White House, cover, 3; AFP/Corbis, 6, 30, 40 (top), 42 (all), 45, 46, 48;
Greg Smith/Corbis SABA, 7; Spencer Platt /Getty Images, 8; George Bush Presidential Library, 9, 10, 12,
13, 16, 17, 20, 54 (left), 56 (left, all); Darren McCollester/Newsmakers/Getty Images, 11, 55 (left);
Bettmann/Corbis, 14, 21, 57 (left); Courtesy Ronald Reagan Library, 18; Owen Franken/Corbis, 19;
Hulton/Archive by Getty Images, 22, 32, 54 (top right), 55 (left, all), 56 (top right); Robert Maass/Corbis,
23; Wally McNamee/Corbis, 24, 58 (top left); F. Carter Smith/Corbis Sygma, 25; Daemmrich Bob/Corbis
Sygma, 26; Newsmakers/Getty Images, 27; Tom Reel/Newsmakers/Getty Images, 28, 58 (bottom left);
Joseph Sohm, Chromosohm Inc./Corbis, 29; Stephen Ferry/Liaison/Getty Images, 31; Pool Photo/
Newsmakers/Getty Images, 33; Chris Hondros/Newsmakers/Getty Images, 34; Mark Wilson/Getty
Images, 36; Reuters NewMedia Inc./Corbis, 37, 38, 50, 59 (left); William Philpott/Reuters/Hulton/
Archive by Getty Images, 39; Reuters/Hulton/Archive by Getty Images, 40 (bottom); Getty Images, 41,
58 (right); Mark Peterson/Corbis SABA, 43; James Tourtellotte/U.S. Customs Service/Getty Images, 44;
Ahmed al Rubayyh/Getty Images, 47; Michael Williams/Newsmakers/Getty Images, 49; Galen Rowell/
Corbis, 54 (bottom right); Bob Krist/Corbis, 56 (bottom right); PhotoDisc, 57 (top right); NASA, 57
(middle right), 59 (bottom right); David & Peter Turnley/Corbis, 57 (bottom right); Digital Vision, 59
(top right)

Editors: E. Russell Primm, Emily J. Dolbear, Melissa McDaniel, and Catherine Neitge
Photo Researcher: Svetlana Zhurkina
Photo Selector: Linda S. Koutris
Designer: The Design Lab
Cartographer: XNR Productions, Inc.

Library of Congress Cataloging-in-Publication Data
Burgan, Michael.
  George W. Bush / by Michael Burgan.
    p. cm. — (Profiles of the presidents)
  Summary: A biography of the forty-third president of United States, which discusses his personal life,
education, and political career.
  Includes bibliographical references and index.
  ISBN 0-7565-0338-8 (alk. paper)
  1. Bush, George W. (George Walker), 1946——Juvenile literature. 2. Presidents—United States—
Biography—Juvenile literature. [1. Bush, George W. (George Walker), 1946– 2. Presidents.] I. Title.
II. Series.
  E903.B86 2004
  973.931'092—dc21   2002156027

Printed in the United States of America.

Table of Contents

★ ★ ★

*NOTE: In this book, words that are defined in the glossary are in **bold** the first time they appear in the text.*

A Historic Election

★ ★ ★

In 2000, George W. Bush won a close race against Vice President Al Gore to become the forty-third president of the United States. When the votes were counted on Election Day, it was not clear who won. The election was finally settled in Florida, where only a few hundred votes separated the two **candidates.** For the first time ever, the U.S. Supreme Court played a role in deciding which candidate won. It took more than a month of arguments before Bush was finally declared the winner.

George W. Bush (left) meets Al Gore in Washington, D.C., for the first time after Bush was declared the winner of the 2000 election.

Bush's victory was historic for another reason.

◄ *George W. Bush (left) and his father, George H. W. Bush*

For the second time in U.S. history, a son followed his father into the presidency. Bush's father, George Herbert Walker Bush, had served as president from 1989 to 1993. The other father-and-son presidents were John Adams and John Quincy Adams, the second and sixth U.S. presidents.

George W. Bush, a Republican, knew that his victory disappointed the Americans who supported Gore. He also knew many voters had questioned his abilities during his **campaign.** Some people wondered if he had enough experience to be a good leader. Bush promised to "unite and inspire the American citizens."

On September 11, 2001, terrorists flew planes into the two towers of the World Trade Center in New York City.

Once in office, Bush faced many problems. Some Americans needed help paying for their medical care. Many believed schools needed to be improved. The U.S. economy was beginning to weaken after several strong years. Those issues, however, faded into the background after September 11, 2001. That day, **terrorist attacks** in New York City, Washington, D.C., and Pennsylvania killed more than three thousand people. The attacks shocked the nation. President Bush then led a war on terrorism. The United States and its allies searched for terrorists who might carry out future attacks. In 2003, the United States launched a successful war against Iraq, a nation in the Middle East. Bush said its ruler, Saddam Hussein, had aided terrorists in the past. Many Americans praised Bush for his strong actions against terrorism. Now it was up to the president to continue to lead America through difficult times.

A Politician's Son

★ ★ ★

George W. Bush followed in the family footsteps when he became a politician. His father had been president, vice president, and a member of Congress. His grand-father Prescott Bush had served in the U.S. Senate. His mother, Barbara, was a distant relative of Franklin Pierce, the fourteenth president of the United States.

George W. Bush was born on July 6, 1946, in New Haven, Connecticut. At the time, his father was attending Yale University. The elder Bush had grown up in nearby Greenwich.

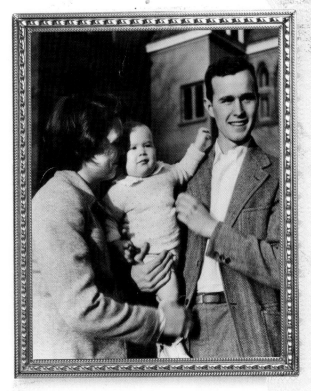

George and Barbara Bush with their first son and future president, George Walker Bush.

*Bush in his ▲
Yale University
baseball uniform*

his life, he showed a good sense of humor and the ability to get along well with others.

Young George often repeated the things his father had done. After graduating from Phillips Academy, he went to Yale University, another school that the elder Bush had attended. He tried out for the baseball team—as his father had—and played his freshman year. He also joined the Skull and Bones, a secret group at Yale to which George H. W. Bush had belonged. Members held private meetings and were not allowed to discuss the business of the club with others.

During Bush's first year in college, his father ran for the U.S. Senate. Young Bush sometimes joined his father on campaign trips. The elder Bush lost that race but won a seat in the U.S. House of Representatives in 1966.

After George W. Bush graduated from Yale in
1968, he returned to Texas and joined the Air National
Guard. He spent a year learning how to be a jet pilot.
At the time, the United States was fighting the Viet-
nam War (1959–1975). Many young men joined the
National Guard to avoid being **drafted** into the military.
Not many guardsmen were sent to fight in Vietnam.
Later, Bush wrote that his years in the National Guard

▼ *Bush (left) joined the
Texas Air National
Guard and served
from 1968 to 1973.*

showed him "the importance of a well-trained and well-equipped military."

Back in Texas, Bush also worked for his father's 1970 campaign for the U.S. Senate. The elder Bush lost that race, but within a year he had a new job—U.S. **ambassador** to the **United Nations.** During the late 1970s, George H. W. Bush became the head of the Central Intelligence Agency (CIA), the major spy organization for the United States.

Ambassador George ▶
H. W. Bush at a
meeting of the United
Nations in 1971

Looking for a Purpose

★ ★ ★

While his father pursued a career in public service, George W. Bush tried to decide what he wanted to do with his life. As he later said, he spent many years "fumbling around." He applied to law school but did not get in. For a time, he worked for free at a Houston organization that helped poor youths stay out of trouble. In 1973, Bush entered Harvard Business School, but he was not sure what he wanted to do even after he earned his master's degree in business administration.

In 1976, Bush returned to Texas. Once again, he followed in his father's footsteps by entering the oil business. The next year, he met and married a school librarian from Midland named Laura Welch. They later had twin daughters, Jenna and Barbara.

Bush made his first run for office in 1978. He became the Republican candidate for a seat in the U.S.

Laura and George W. Bush with their twin daughters, Barbara (left) and Jenna, in 1987

House of Representatives, but he lost the race to a Democrat. Bush decided to stay out of politics for a while and focus instead on the oil business.

Bush set up his own company. He called it Arbusto, which is Spanish for "bush" or "shrub." Later, he renamed the company Bush Exploration. He did well at first, raising $3 million from investors and finding oil.

By the mid-1980s, however, the price of oil was falling, and the company began to struggle. Bush sold his company to a larger business. A few years later, he left the oil industry for good.

▼ *Bush speaking to workers in an oil field at the time he founded Arbusto*

During these years, Bush's father was serving as vice president of the United States under President Ronald Reagan. They had been elected in 1980. As president, Ronald Reagan brought many **conservative** ideas to the White House. He wanted to cut taxes and limit the role of the government in business. Reagan also wanted to strengthen the U.S. military. Vice President Bush accepted Reagan's policies, even though he had not been a strong conservative before becoming vice president.

In 1988, Bush's father decided to run for president. George W. Bush took time off from work to help run his father's campaign. "I was a warrior for George Bush," he later wrote. "I would do anything for my

President Ronald ▶
Reagan (left) and Vice
President George H. W.
Bush in July 1981

dad." The elder Bush said he wanted to continue Reagan's conservative policies. Some Republicans, however, did not think Bush was a true conservative. They worried he would reject some of Reagan's policies if he won the election. George W. Bush tried to convince these conservatives that his father shared their beliefs.

A born-again Christian raising his arms in worship during a religious service

The younger Bush focused on convincing born-again Christians to support his father. Born-again Christians are

George H. W. ▶
Bush being
sworn in as
president in
January 1989

people who have renewed their faith in Jesus Christ, often because of a strong religious experience. Bush had become a born-again Christian during the 1980s.

During his father's successful presidential campaign, Bush also tried to make sure reporters and politicians did not say or write anything bad about his father. Bush expected people around his father to be loyal. He demanded the same loyalty from his friends and aides when he entered politics.

Governor Bush

★ ★ ★

George W. Bush learned a lot about politics during his father's presidential campaign. When he returned to Texas, some reporters wondered if he would run for office him-self. Bush knew, though, that Texans would not elect him unless he achieved some success on his own. That chance came in 1989, when he became part owner of the Texas Rangers base-ball team.

▼ George W. Bush was part owner of the Texas Rangers baseball team.

Bush and the Rangers con-vinced officials in Arlington, Texas, to build the team a new stadium. Bush often attended home games. Because he was the president's son, his picture usually turned up on TV broadcasts of the games. When the team was sold in 1998, Bush made a profit

Bill Clinton (left) and George H. W. Bush at the White House shortly after Clinton's victory in the presidential election of 1992

of about $15 million. Owning the Rangers also had another advantage. Bush wrote, "Baseball was a great training ground for politics and government. The bottom line in baseball is results: wins and losses."

In 1992, Bush's father ran for reelection but lost to Bill Clinton. By that time, the younger Bush was thinking about running for office, too. In 1994, he planned to challenge Democratic incumbent Ann Richards in the upcoming election for governor of Texas.

Richards was a popular governor, and Texans had rarely elected a Republican to the job. Still, Bush had plenty of support among business owners and his father's friends. He ran as a conservative, stressing the need for people to help themselves. Bush believed people should not rely on the government for aid. "All public policy," he told one crowd, "should revolve around the principle that individuals are responsible for what they say and do."

▲ *Texas governor Ann Richards in 1992*

Bush won the governor's race by more than three hundred thousand votes. His personality helped him win support. In small groups, he talked easily with voters and showed concern about their problems. He also spoke Spanish, which helped him win votes from the state's large Hispanic population.

As governor, Bush tried to appeal to both Democrats and Republicans. For Republicans, he lowered taxes and helped poor people receiving government aid find jobs. He also insisted on dealing harshly with criminals. For Democrats, he stressed spending more money on education. Bush began calling himself a "compassionate conservative" who would take care of the needy while pursuing conservative policies.

In 1998, Bush ran for governor again and made education his key issue. He promised to keep improving the state's schools. At the same time, he kept close contact with business owners and conservative Republicans. One issue popular with conservatives—his strong support for the death penalty—became important in the campaign.

For the first time in more than one hundred years, Texas was about to **execute** a woman for committing a crime. A drug addict named Karla Fay Tucker had killed two people in 1983 and was sentenced to death. During her many years in prison, she became a born-again Christian. By the time Tucker was supposed to be executed, many groups across America came to her

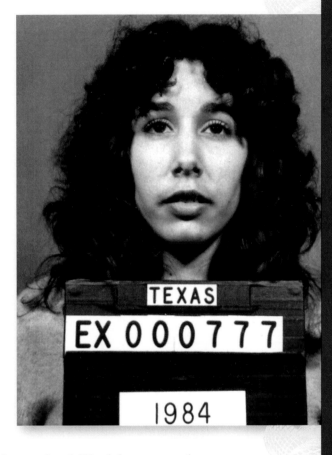

▲ *Karla Fay Tucker was at the center of a huge debate over the death penalty.*

defense. They said she should not be killed because she was not the same person she had been in 1983. Others defended her because they did not believe in the death penalty. These different groups asked Bush to spare Tucker's life—a legal right he had as governor. Bush refused. He later said, "My job is to uphold the law of the land. . . . My job is not to judge hearts." The debate over Tucker's execution gained Bush national attention.

The 1998 governor's race also drew attention to Bush's past. Some people claimed he had used drugs, including cocaine, as a young man. Bush refused to say what he had done in college or the years after. He admitted he had done some things he was not proud of and that he used to drink too much alcohol. He said all of that was in the past. Despite these questions, Bush easily won reelection.

George W. Bush ▶ and his wife, Laura, watching the televised election results from the 1998 race for governor

Rough Road to the White House

★   ★   ★

After his big victory in Texas, Bush began preparing to run for president in 2000. He had several problems to overcome. In his speeches, he sometimes misused or made up words. Some reporters and political experts claimed he was not smart enough to be president. Others said he did not focus on the details of running a government. Bush's supporters disagreed and explained that once he had made a decision, he preferred to let his aides work out the details of the plan.

▼ Confetti and balloons fell on George W. Bush as he accepted the Republican Party's nomination to run for president in the 2000 election.

Laura and George ▲
W. Bush (left) and
Dick and Lynne
Cheney wave to the
press in Austin,
Texas, in July 2000.

Even though some people questioned his skills, there were several factors in Bush's favor during the election. He was the son of a former president, and he could count on the support of many wealthy Republicans. As his campaign went on, Bush raised $93 million—more than any other U.S. presidential candidate in history. This money helped him hire talented people and allowed him to put many ads on television. Bush also came across as likable and as someone people could trust.

Bush beat several other Republicans to become his party's candidate for president. He chose Dick Cheney as his running mate. Cheney had served as secretary of defense when Bush's father was president.

The Democratic candidate for president in 2000 was Vice President Al Gore. The vice president tried to win votes by saying that the Democrats had just led the country through a great economic boom. He promised to keep the economy strong. He also claimed that he had more experience and a better understanding of important issues than Bush. However, Gore had problems to overcome, as well. Many people considered him dull and stiff when he spoke in public.

▼ *Democratic presidential candidate Al Gore promised to keep the economy strong.*

During the campaign, Bush continued to stress that he was a compassionate conservative. "It is conservative to cut taxes," he said. "It is compassionate to help people save and give and build." Bush wanted private organizations and churches to do more for the needy, instead of the government being directly involved. He also called for spending more money on the military and building a missile defense system. This system would use small missiles to destroy any large missiles launched at the United States.

On Election Day, Gore beat Bush by more than half a million votes. However, a presidential race is not decided by the total number of votes cast. It is instead decided by electoral votes. Each state has a number of electoral votes, based on the number of representatives it has in the U.S. Congress. In every state except Maine and Nebraska, the candidate who receives the most votes wins all of that

The radar panel (left) is part of a laser weapon used to track and destroy enemy missiles. During his 2000 presidential campiagn, Bush emphasized the need for this type of missile defense system.

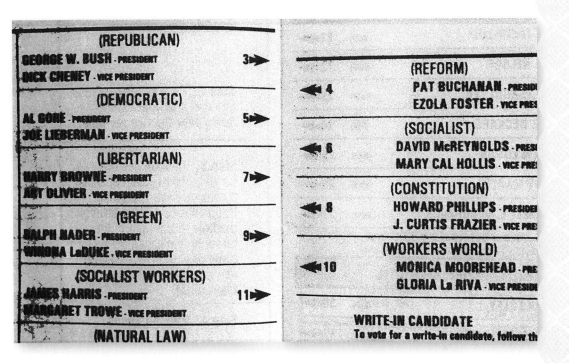

(REPUBLICAN)
GEORGE W. BUSH - PRESIDENT   3➤
DICK CHENEY - VICE PRESIDENT

(DEMOCRATIC)
AL GORE - PRESIDENT   5➤
JOE LIEBERMAN - VICE PRESIDENT

(LIBERTARIAN)
HARRY BROWNE - PRESIDENT   7➤
ART OLIVIER - VICE PRESIDENT

(GREEN)
RALPH NADER - PRESIDENT   9➤
WINONA LaDUKE - VICE PRESIDENT

(SOCIALIST WORKERS)
JAMES HARRIS - PRESIDENT   11➤
MARGARET TROWE - VICE PRESIDENT

(NATURAL LAW)

◄ 4   **(REFORM)**
PAT BUCHANAN - PRESIDE
EZOLA FOSTER - VICE PRES

◄ 6   **(SOCIALIST)**
DAVID McREYNOLDS - PRESI
MARY CAL HOLLIS - VICE PRE

◄ 8   **(CONSTITUTION)**
HOWARD PHILLIPS - PRESIDE
J. CURTIS FRAZIER - VICE PRE

◄ 10   **(WORKERS WORLD)**
MONICA MOOREHEAD - PRE
GLORIA La RIVA - VICE PRESIDE

WRITE-IN CANDIDATE
To vote for a write-in candidate, follow th

A ballot used in Palm Beach County, Florida, to cast a vote in the 2000 presidential election

state's electoral votes. In 2000, the electoral vote was extremely close. Each candidate needed to win Florida to become president. At first, Bush seemed to have a slim lead in Florida, but the results were not clear.

The election had not gone smoothly in Florida. In some cities, voting machines did not work properly. In other places, voters were confused by the way the candidates' names were listed on the ballots. Some people claimed they had mistakenly voted for someone other than who they really wanted. With all the confusion, Gore requested a recount of some votes.

Bush's younger ▶
brother, Jeb,
the governor
of Florida

There were also political questions about the Florida results. Bush's brother Jeb was the state's governor. The woman in charge of the Florida election, Secretary of State Katherine Harris, was also a strong supporter of George W. Bush. Democrats argued that Harris and Jeb Bush would not be fair to Gore.

By state law, Harris had to declare a winner within seven days of the election. The recounts, however, were not finished in that time. After a week, Bush was ahead by several hundred votes. Then Gore won a major legal victory. The Florida Supreme Court said the final result must include all of the recounted votes, even if state officials needed more than seven days to count them.

Bush decided to take the issue to the U.S. Supreme Court. On December 12, the U.S. Supreme Court ruled

▾ Florida Secretary of State Katherine Harris in November 2000

The New York Times

BUSH PREVAILS

BY SINGLE VOTE, JUSTICES END RECOUNT,
BLOCKING GORE AFTER 5-WEEK STRUGGLE

An Awareness of Hazards

DAILY NEWS
HISTORIC RULING
BUSH WINS
U.S. SUPREME COURT
REJECTS FLA. RECOUNT
COMPLETE ELECTION COVERAGE BEGINS ON PAGES 2-3

Newspaper headlines on December 13, 2000, reported Bush's victory a day after the U.S. Supreme Court ruled in his favor on the issue of the Florida recounts.

that the Florida Supreme Court decision to allow the recounts was incorrect. Gore decided to stop his legal challenge, and Florida's electoral votes were awarded to Bush. Bush ended up with 271 electoral votes—just one more than he needed to win the election. Bush became the fourth president to be elected without winning the most votes at the polls. (The others were John Quincy Adams, Rutherford B. Hayes, and Benjamin Harrison.)

When choosing his top advisers, President Bush turned to some of the people who had worked with his father. The new secretary of state, Colin Powell, had served as the chairman of the Joint Chiefs of Staff—the president's top military adviser—under former presidents George H. W. Bush and Bill Clinton. As secretary of state, Powell would help shape U.S. policy toward other countries. Another important adviser for both Bushes was Condoleezza Rice. Powell and Rice joined Cheney and Secretary of Defense Donald Rumsfeld as Bush's top aides in dealing with foreign nations.

Early in his presidency, Bush focused on issues at home. He called for a tax cut worth more than $1 trillion.

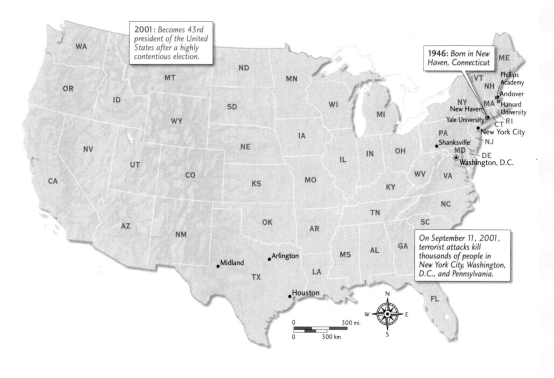

2001: Becomes 43rd president of the United States after a highly contentious election.

1946: Born in New Haven, Connecticut

Phillips Academy Andover

Harvard University

New Haven

Yale University

New York City

Shanksville

Washington, D.C.

On September 11, 2001, terrorist attacks kill thousands of people in New York City, Washington, D.C., and Pennsylvania.

Midland

Arlington

Houston

0   300 mi.
0   300 km

Vice President Dick Cheney (left), Secretary of State Colin Powell, President George W. Bush, and National Security Adviser Condoleezza Rice during a meeting at the White House

"Let's get as much as possible for the American people," he told reporters. Bush claimed people would use the money they saved in taxes to invest in businesses and buy more products—steps that would help build up the economy.

Bush also wanted fewer government limits on some businesses. He hoped to end certain laws that protected the environment because he said they hurt business. Bush was against an international treaty, or agreement, signed in Kyoto, Japan, in 1997. The treaty called on wealthy nations, such as the United States, to produce less of certain gases thought to harm the environment. Bush said cutting the production of these gases would cost U.S. companies too much money.

Defense was another key issue Bush tackled early in his presidency. He promised to spend more on weapons and to increase soldiers' wages. He also promoted a new missile defense system. Bush supported the new missiles even though building them would mean ending a treaty between the United States and Russia. Signed in 1972, the treaty limited the kind of missile defense system each

◀ *Protesters in Tokyo, Japan, demonstrate against American rejection of the Kyoto treaty.*

country could build. Bush said protecting the United States was more important than honoring the treaty.

As president, Bush had to make important decisions every day. He enjoyed the challenge of running the most powerful nation in the world. He told a group of business leaders, "It's hard to describe the honor I feel every morning, walking into the **Oval Office.**" To deal with the pressure, he relied on his sense of humor. He also stayed active, jogging and working out in the White House weight room. Bush trusted his aides to carry out his decisions. He was confident he could do the job he was elected to do. Bush could not have imagined how difficult that job would become, however, after the events of just one day.

President Bush ▾ entering the Oval Office

September 11 and Beyond

★ ★ ★

On the morning of September 11, 2001, President Bush was visiting an elementary school in Florida. While he was there, he learned that a plane had crashed into one of the twin towers of New York City's World Trade Center. Another plane hit the second tower just a few minutes later. Bush and his aides knew the crashes were not accidents—America was under attack. Within an hour, a third plane crashed into the Pentagon, the headquarters of the Defense Department near Washington, D.C. A fourth plane crashed into a field in

▾ The Pentagon after an airplane crashed into it on September 11, 2001

Pennsylvania. Later, the country learned this plane had been heading to Washington, D.C., to strike the U.S. Capitol or another government building.

More than three thousand people died in these crashes. All four planes had been **hijacked** by small groups of Arab men. The hijackings were part of a terrorist plot against the United States. The man behind the plot was Osama bin Laden.

Bin Laden belonged to a wealthy family from Saudi Arabia. He was a Muslim—a follower of the Islamic religion. He practiced

Osama bin Laden ▲ planned the terrorist attacks that occurred on September 11, 2001.

Members of al ▶ Qaeda after they were captured in the Tora Bora Mountains of Afghanistan in December 2001

a strict form of Islam that dislikes modern society. Bin Laden blamed the United States and its **allies** for many of the world's problems. He used his riches to recruit and train Islamic terrorists who accepted his beliefs. His group, called al Qaeda, had carried out earlier attacks against Americans and U.S. property. The September 11 attacks were the worst terrorist acts ever against the United States.

After September 11, Bush said the United States was at war. However, the war was with an enemy who was hard to find. Al Qaeda is divided into small groups of followers,

Khalid Shaikh Mohammed

◄ An FBI poster of Khalid Shaikh Mohammed, who was arrested in March 2003 in connection with the September 11 terrorist attacks

called cells, all around the world. The terrorists live as normal citizens until it is time to carry out an attack.

Bush began planning an attack against bin Laden and al Qaeda. Officials believed bin Laden was operating out of Afghanistan, a country in central Asia. Afghanistan was ruled by the Taliban, a group that shared bin Laden's views. Bush called on other countries to join the United States in its fight against the terrorists. These allies would

British Prime Minister Tony Blair (left) and President Bush discuss U.S. and British military operations.

U.S. soldiers on duty at an air base in Afghanistan in December 2001.

help U.S. forces in Afghanistan. They would also hunt
for al Qaeda cells in their
own lands.

In October, American and
British forces began attacking
Taliban forces in Afghanistan.
By the end of December, the
Taliban was forced out of
power. Several of al Qaeda's
camps had been destroyed.
Bin Laden, however, had
managed to escape.

▲ *An airport security
guard (left) inspects a
passenger's luggage
at John F. Kennedy
International Airport
in New York City.
After September 11,
2001, airline security
was increased across
the country.*

As the fight against terrorism continued, Bush looked
for ways to track down terrorists already in the United
States. He also wanted to prevent more terrorists from
entering the country. Security at airports, power plants, and
government buildings was increased. The U.S. government
rounded up thousands of **immigrants** who might have been
in the country illegally or who may have possibly had ties
to terrorists.

In November 2002, Congress created the Department
of Homeland Security. This new department combined

Tom Ridge became ▶
the leader of Bush's
new Department of
Homeland Security.

many government organizations into one agency that
worked to protect Americans. Bush told the nation,
"We're fighting a war against terror with all our
resources, and we're determined to win."

Not everyone liked what Bush was doing. Some
Americans feared the war on terror was weakening the
legal rights of both U.S. citizens and legal immigrants.
They attacked a government plan that asked postal
workers and others who dealt with the public to report
unusual activity. The plan was quickly dropped. Even

some Bush supporters thought the government was trying to record too much private information about average Americans.

As the war on terror continued, Bush and others worried that future attacks could be even deadlier than September 11. In the past, bin Laden had tried to obtain powerful bombs and weapons that use deadly chem-

▼ *Foreign reporters inspect Iraqi missiles near Baghdad, Iraq, in 2003. Bush feared that Iraq might supply bin Laden with powerful weapons.*

icals or diseases to kill thousands of people at once. Bush thought bin Laden or other terrorists might get weapons from Iraq.

In 1991, President George H. W. Bush had led a war against Iraq after that country invaded its neighbor, Kuwait. Iraq's leader, Saddam Hussein, had remained a U.S. enemy ever since. At times, he even attacked his

Iraqi girls march in front of a painting of Iraqi President Saddam Hussein during his birthday celebration in 2001.

own people. He also developed weapons of mass destruction. After Iraq lost the war in 1991, United Nations inspectors searched the country for these weapons and destroyed what they found. The inspectors left Iraq in 1998. However, George W. Bush was convinced Hussein still had powerful weapons and was building more. The president worried that Hussein would give the weapons to terrorists or use them himself against the United States and its allies.

▲ *In November 2002, United Nations inspectors depart from a site near Baghdad that was once used to develop missiles and possibly other powerful weapons.*

Bush said Iraq must give up these weapons. He demanded that the United Nations inspectors return to Iraq to search for more weapons. If Iraq refused to allow this, Bush was ready to attack. In November 2002, Iraq let the inspectors return. After several months, the inspectors did not find any weapons of mass destruction. The U.S. government, however, said it had information that Iraq was hiding these weapons. In March 2003, the United States and several allies invaded Iraq. Some Americans, and many people around the world, opposed this war. Bush said, however, that the fighting would protect the United States. In just four weeks, U.S. and British troops forced Saddam from power and began setting up a new government. President Bush told Americans, "You and I and all the world are witnessing historic days in the cause of freedom."

The Iraqi oil ministry building in Baghdad burns after being hit during a U.S. air raid in March 2003.

Looking to the Future

★　★　★

Terrorists and Iraq were not President Bush's only concerns. At home, he focused on more tax cuts to help the worsening economy. He continued to stress improving education. He also made it easier for companies to mine, drill for oil, and cut down trees on government lands.

▾ First Lady Laura Bush reads to elementary students in Whitehall, Ohio, to help emphasize her husband's belief in the need to improve education.

During his presidency, Bush welcomed more countries into the North Atlantic Treaty Organization (NATO). This military organization was started by the United States in 1949. Each country in NATO promises to help defend other members if they come under attack. Bush said NATO would help defeat terrorists, whom he called "the new enemies of freedom."

As Bush continued his presidency, he knew the United States faced many challenges. "At this moment in history," he said, "if there is a world problem, we're expected to deal with it [and] . . . we will."

President George W. Bush salutes members of the U.S. Marine Corps at Fort Lejeune, North Carolina, during the U.S. war against Iraq in 2003.

GLOSSARY

★ ★ ★

allies—countries that support one another in a conflict

ambassador—the representative of a nation's government in another country

campaign—a series of efforts to win an election

candidates—people running for office in an election

conservative—believing that the government should have a limited role in people's lives

drafted—forced to serve in the military

execute—to put a person to death as punishment for a crime

hijacked—taken over by force

immigrants—people who move from one country to live permanently in another

Oval Office—the president's office in the White House

terrorist attacks—acts committed by people who use violence and fear to further their cause

United Nations—an organization of nations from around the world that tries to settle disputes between countries

GEORGE W. BUSH'S LIFE AT A GLANCE

★ ★ ★

PERSONAL

Nickname:	W. (Dub-ya)
Birth date:	July 6, 1946
Birthplace:	New Haven, Connecticut
Father's name:	George Herbert Walker Bush
Mother's name:	Barbara Pierce Bush
Education:	Graduated from Yale University in 1968 and Harvard Business School in 1975
Wife's name:	Laura Welch Bush (1946–)
Married:	November 5, 1977
Children:	Barbara Pierce Bush (1981–); Jenna Welch Bush (1981–)

PUBLIC

Occupation before presidency: Businessman

Military service: Member of the Air National Guard (1968–1973)

Other government positions: Governor of Texas

Political party: Republican

Vice president: Richard Cheney (2001–)

Dates in office: January 20, 2001–

Presidential opponent: Albert Gore Jr. (Democrat), 2000

Number of votes (Electoral College): 50,456,167 of 101,452,231 (271 of 537)

Writings: *A Charge to Keep* (1999)

★

George W. Bush's Cabinet

Secretary of state:
 Colin Powell (2001–)

Secretary of the treasury:
 Paul O'Neill (2001–2002)
 John Snow (2003–)

Secretary of defense:
 Donald H. Rumsfeld (2001–)

Attorney general:
 John Ashcroft (2001–)

Secretary of the interior:
 Gale Norton (2001–)

Secretary of agriculture:
 Ann Veneman (2001–)

Secretary of commerce:
 Don Evans (2001–)

Secretary of labor:
 Elaine Chao (2001–)

Secretary of health and human services:
 Tommy G. Thompson (2001–)

Secretary of housing and urban development:
 Mel Martinez (2001–)

Secretary of transportation:
 Norman Y. Mineta (2001–)

Secretary of energy:
 Spencer Abraham (2001–)

Secretary of education:
 Roderick R. Paige (2001–)

Secretary of veterans affairs:
 Anthony Principi (2001–)

Secretary of homeland security:
 Tom Ridge (2002–)

GEORGE W. BUSH'S LIFE AND TIMES

★ ★ ★

BUSH'S LIFE

WORLD EVENTS

1945 America drops atomic bombs on the Japanese cities of Hiroshima and Nagasaki to end World War II (1939–1945)

The United Nations (below) is founded

July 6, George W. Bush is born in New Haven, Connecticut   1946

1950

1949 Birth of the People's Republic of China

1953 The first Europeans climb Mount Everest (below)

BUSH'S LIFE

WORLD EVENTS

1960

1959   Fidel Castro (below)
becomes prime
minister of Cuba

Enters Phillips   1961
Academy (below)
in Andover,
Massachusetts

1961   Soviet cosmonaut
Yuri Gagarin (right)
is the first human to
enter space

The Berlin Wall
(below) is built,
dividing East and
West Germany

1963   Dr. Martin Luther
King Jr. delivers his "I
Have a Dream" speech
to more than 250,000
people attending the
March on Washington

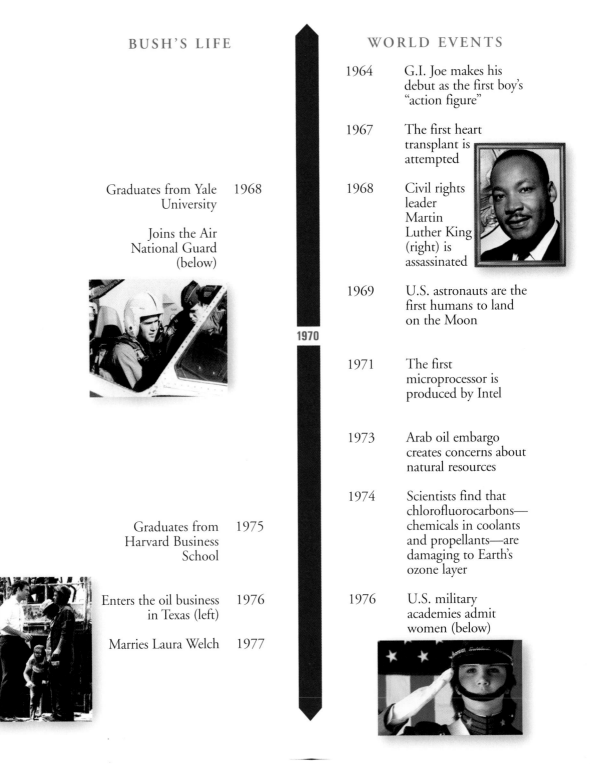

BUSH'S LIFE

Graduates from Yale 1968
University

Joins the Air
National Guard
(below)

Graduates from 1975
Harvard Business
School

Enters the oil business 1976
in Texas (left)

Marries Laura Welch 1977

WORLD EVENTS

1964   G.I. Joe makes his debut as the first boy's "action figure"

1967   The first heart transplant is attempted

1968   Civil rights leader Martin Luther King (right) is assassinated

1969   U.S. astronauts are the first humans to land on the Moon

1970

1971   The first microprocessor is produced by Intel

1973   Arab oil embargo creates concerns about natural resources

1974   Scientists find that chlorofluorocarbons— chemicals in coolants and propellants—are damaging to Earth's ozone layer

1976   U.S. military academies admit women (below)

BUSH'S LIFE

WORLD EVENTS

1980

1982   Maya Lin designs the
Vietnam Veterans
Memorial (right),
commemorating the
Americans who died

1983   The AIDS (acquired
immune deficiency
syndrome) virus is
identified

1986   The U.S. space
shuttle *Challenger*
explodes (right),
killing all seven
astronauts on board

Works on George   1988
H. W. Bush's
campaign for president

Becomes part owner of   1989
the Texas Rangers
baseball team

1990   1990   Political prisoner
Nelson Mandela
(right), a leader of
the antiapartheid
movement in South
Africa, is released;
Mandela becomes
president of South
Africa in 1994

1991   The Soviet Union
collapses and is
replaced by the
Commonwealth of
Independent States

The United States
leads international
forces in an effort to
drive Iraqi forces out
of Kuwait

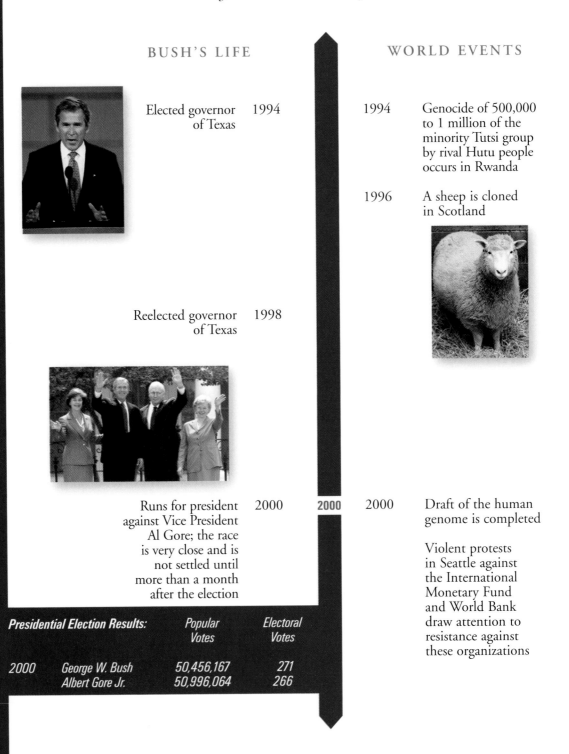

BUSH'S LIFE

WORLD EVENTS

Elected governor of Texas — 1994

1994 — Genocide of 500,000 to 1 million of the minority Tutsi group by rival Hutu people occurs in Rwanda

1996 — A sheep is cloned in Scotland

Reelected governor of Texas — 1998

Runs for president against Vice President Al Gore; the race is very close and is not settled until more than a month after the election — 2000

2000

2000 — Draft of the human genome is completed

Violent protests in Seattle against the International Monetary Fund and World Bank draw attention to resistance against these organizations

Presidential Election Results:	Popular Votes	Electoral Votes
2000 George W. Bush	50,456,167	271
Albert Gore Jr.	50,996,064	266

BUSH'S LIFE

Opposes international 　2001
Kyoto Treaty that
would protect the
environment

American and British
troops attack Taliban
forces in Afghanistan

Congress creates the 　2002
Department of
Homeland Security

The United States and 　2003
its allies invade Iraq;
Saddam Hussein's
regime falls

WORLD EVENTS

2001　Terrorist attacks on
the two World Trade
Center towers (below)
in New York City and
on the Pentagon in
Washington, D.C.,
leave thousands dead

2003　The U.S. space
shuttle *Columbia*
explodes, killing all
seven astronauts on
board (below)

UNDERSTANDING GEORGE W. BUSH AND HIS PRESIDENCY

★ ★ ★

IN THE LIBRARY

Currie, Stephen. *Terrorists and Terror Groups.*
San Diego: Lucent Books, 2002.

Hamilton, John. *Operation Enduring Freedom.*
Edina, Minn.: Abdo Publishing, 2002.

McNeese, Tim. *George W. Bush: First President of the New Century.*
Greensboro, N.C.: Morgan Reynolds, 2002.

Shields, Charles. *Saddam Hussein.* Philadelphia: Chelsea House, 2002.

ON THE WEB

2000 Election Chronology
http://www.infoplease.com/ipa/A0884144.html
For a timeline and more information on the presidential election
of 2000 and the disputed results in Florida

The American Presidency—George W. Bush
http://gi.grolier.com/presidents/ea/bios/43pgwb.html
To read a biography of George W. Bush and his inaugural address

Internet Public Library—George W. Bush
http://www.potus.com/gwbush.html
For information about Bush's presidency
and many links to other resources

September 11 News.com
http://www.september11news.com/
For links to sites with photos and news reports
on the September 11 terrorist attacks

The White House—George W. Bush
http://www.whitehouse.gov/
For the latest news on the president's activities and public statements

BUSH HISTORIC SITES
ACROSS THE COUNTRY

Texas State Capitol
Capitol Visitors Center
112 East 11th Street
Austin, TX 78701
512/463-5495
To learn about Bush's role in Texas government

The White House
1600 Pennsylvania Avenue NW
Washington, D.C. 20500
202/456-1111
To see where Bush lives and works

THE U.S. PRESIDENTS
(Years in Office)

★ ★ ★

1. **George Washington**
   (March 4, 1789-March 3, 1797)
2. **John Adams**
   (March 4, 1797-March 3, 1801)
3. **Thomas Jefferson**
   (March 4, 1801-March 3, 1809)
4. **James Madison**
   (March 4, 1809-March 3, 1817)
5. **James Monroe**
   (March 4, 1817-March 3, 1825)
6. **John Quincy Adams**
   (March 4, 1825-March 3, 1829)
7. **Andrew Jackson**
   (March 4, 1829-March 3, 1837)
8. **Martin Van Buren**
   (March 4, 1837-March 3, 1841)
9. **William Henry Harrison**
   (March 6, 1841-April 4, 1841)
10. **John Tyler**
    (April 6, 1841-March 3, 1845)
11. **James K. Polk**
    (March 4, 1845-March 3, 1849)
12. **Zachary Taylor**
    (March 5, 1849-July 9, 1850)
13. **Millard Fillmore**
    (July 10, 1850-March 3, 1853)
14. **Franklin Pierce**
    (March 4, 1853-March 3, 1857)
15. **James Buchanan**
    (March 4, 1857-March 3, 1861)
16. **Abraham Lincoln**
    (March 4, 1861-April 15, 1865)
17. **Andrew Johnson**
    (April 15, 1865-March 3, 1869)

18. **Ulysses S. Grant**
    (March 4, 1869-March 3, 1877)
19. **Rutherford B. Hayes**
    (March 4, 1877-March 3, 1881)
20. **James Garfield**
    (March 4, 1881-Sept 19, 1881)
21. **Chester Arthur**
    (Sept 20, 1881-March 3, 1885)
22. **Grover Cleveland**
    (March 4, 1885-March 3, 1889)
23. **Benjamin Harrison**
    (March 4, 1889-March 3, 1893)
24. **Grover Cleveland**
    (March 4, 1893-March 3, 1897)
25. **William McKinley**
    (March 4, 1897-
    September 14, 1901)
26. **Theodore Roosevelt**
    (September 14, 1901-
    March 3, 1909)
27. **William Howard Taft**
    (March 4, 1909-March 3, 1913)
28. **Woodrow Wilson**
    (March 4, 1913-March 3, 1921)
29. **Warren G. Harding**
    (March 4, 1921-August 2, 1923)
30. **Calvin Coolidge**
    (August 3, 1923-March 3, 1929)
31. **Herbert Hoover**
    (March 4, 1929-March 3, 1933)
32. **Franklin D. Roosevelt**
    (March 4, 1933-April 12, 1945)

33. **Harry S. Truman**
    (April 12, 1945-
    January 20, 1953)
34. **Dwight D. Eisenhower**
    (January 20, 1953-
    January 20, 1961)
35. **John F. Kennedy**
    (January 20, 1961-
    November 22, 1963)
36. **Lyndon B. Johnson**
    (November 22, 1963-
    January 20, 1969)
37. **Richard M. Nixon**
    (January 20, 1969-
    August 9, 1974)
38. **Gerald R. Ford**
    (August 9, 1974-
    January 20, 1977)
39. **James Earl Carter**
    (January 20, 1977-
    January 20, 1981)
40. **Ronald Reagan**
    (January 20, 1981-
    January 20, 1989)
41. **George H. W. Bush**
    (January 20, 1989-
    January 20, 1993)
42. **William Jefferson Clinton**
    (January 20, 1993-
    January 20, 2001)
43. George W. Bush
    (January 20, 2001-)

INDEX

★ ★ ★

ABOUT THE AUTHOR

Michael Burgan is a freelance writer of books for children and adults. A history graduate of the University of Connecticut, he has written more than thirty fiction and nonfiction children's books for various publishers. For adult audiences, he has written news articles, essays, and plays. Michael Burgan is a recipient of an Edpress Award and belongs to the Society of Children's Book Writers and Illustrators.